The Foun[c] American G[c]

The rioting and looting following [...] popular court decision sent shock waves throughout the nation, but then the rioting and looting following a victorious basketball game served to illustrate the sobering fact that criminal behavior is out of control in America. There is hope, however, if these tragic events force us to return to the Biblical foundation of our nation and to the understanding of its positive benefits on society.

Our form of government has become pre-eminent among those in the world, and it is our Constitution which has helped bring this nation to a position rarely rivaled by any nation in the last two centuries. Our Constitution is enhanced by a Bill of Rights, whereby the rights and liberties of individuals and states are protected. Although both of these documents have had great impact on the nation, ironically, the greatest impact felt on American government in recent years has been from something not found in either founding document: it has been from the phrase "separation of church and state."

A conversation I had with a U.S. Congressman who is an accomplished attorney illustrated the power of this phrase. We were discussing the importance of religious values in public affairs. He stated, "We know they're important; we just can't do anything about it."

I asked, "Why not?"

He replied, "Well, we just can't."

I persisted, "Why?"

He answered, "Because of 'separation of church and state'—we cannot have religious values in public affairs."

I questioned him, "'Separation of church and state'; where is that?"

He replied, "It's in the Constitution—the Constitution won't let us do it."

I responded, "That's not in the Constitution."

He said, "Yes, it is."

---

* EDITOR'S NOTE: This is a partially edited version of the video cassette and audio tape "Foundations of American Government" (also called, "What the Founding Fathers Really Meant by 'Separation of Church and State'"), © 1992, by David Barton, all rights reserved. The slight edit is needed because sometimes things communicated verbally do not communicate the same message in written form. Nonetheless, the content and message of this printed format is substantially the same as the tape.

"No, it's not."

"Yes, it is." We went back and forth; then I gave him a copy of the Constitution and asked, "Would you please find that phrase for me?"

He said, "I'd be happy to"; and he immediately went to the First Amendment, read it and became very embarrassed. He said, "I can't believe this! In law school they always taught us that's what the First Amendment said."

I asked him, "You've never read the Constitution for yourself?"

He replied, "We were never required to read it in law school."

This expresses the dilemma we now have in America. Although the phrase "separation of church and state" is well known and commonly associated with the First Amendment, the First Amendment states that "Congress shall make no law respecting an establishment of religion, or prohibiting the free exercise thereof." The words "separation," "church," or "state" are not only not found in the First Amendment, they are found in no founding document!

Still, many, after learning that the phrase is not present, frequently ask, "Well, even though the words aren't there, isn't that what the First Amendment really means?" According to the Founding Fathers and their discussions of the First Amendment which are recorded in the *Congressional Records* from June 7 to September 25, 1789 [1] (the period in which they framed the First Amendment), the Founders explained clearly and succinctly that all they wanted to preclude was what they had experienced in Great Britain. They did not want the establishment—by the federal government—of one single denomination in exclusion of all others, whether that would be Catholic, or Anglican, or any other denomination; there was not going to be—by government decree—one national denomination in America. That is why the wording in the First Amendment prohibits Congress from an establishment of religion—or in the words proposed by James Madison, "the establishment of a national religion." [2]

The meaning of the Founders' word "religion" in the First Amendment has changed dramatically from its original usage, causing us today to misunderstand and misapply their original intent. The word "religion" in the Founders' First Amendment discussions was used to mean a single Christian denomination—a fact made evident by the dozen or so different iterations of the First Amendment which they proposed.

The original version proposed in the Senate on September 3, 1789, stated, "Congress shall not make any law establishing any religious

The Foundations of American Government

A Transcript
of the Video and Audio
by the Same Title

by

David Barton

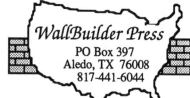

WallBuilder Press
PO Box 397
Aledo, TX 76008
817-441-6044

Nehemiah 2:17: "You see the distress that we
are in . . . come, let us build the walls
that we may no longer be a reproach."

WallBuilder Press
P.O. Box 397
Aledo, Texas 76008
817-441-6044

Printed in the United States of America
ISBN 0-925279-32-3

denomination." Their second version stated, "Congress shall make no law establishing any particular denomination." The third version was very similar, "Congress shall make no law establishing any particular denomination in preference to others." The final version passed on that day declared, "Congress shall make no law establishing religion or prohibiting the free exercise thereof" [3]—wording almost identical to the final wording agreed upon between the House and the Senate. You see, according to their records, the word "religion" was interchangeable with "denomination."

Although the Founding Fathers did not want a single denomination to rule America, they did expect basic Biblical principles and values to remain integral. Just as the Founders forcefully opposed any establishment of a national denomination, they equally forcefully opposed any separation of Biblical principles or values from society or public affairs. For example, consider Fisher Ames.

According to the *Congressional Records,* on September 20, 1789, Fisher Ames was the Founding Father who offered the final wording for the First Amendment; [4] certainly, therefore, he understood the intent of the First Amendment. In an article written for a national magazine in January of 1801, Fisher Ames expressed concern that as more and more books were being introduced into school classrooms, the Bible might someday drift to the back of the classroom. He warned that this could never be allowed in America and that the Bible must always remain the number one textbook in our schools. He urged:

> "Why then, if these [new] books for children must be retained, as they will be, should not the Bible regain the place it once held as a school book?" [5]

Fisher Ames concluded by stressing that the Bible was the source of sound morality and behavior in America [6] and that we must never let it be separated from the classroom. Clearly, the use of the Bible in schools did not violate Fisher Ames' view of the First Amendment—and he was the Founding Father who provided the wording for the First Amendment!

Founding Father Benjamin Rush was not only a signer of the Declaration of Independence, he served in three presidential administrations—under Presidents John Adams, Thomas Jefferson, and James Madison. He was a great policy maker; he was America's leading educator; and he was the first Founding Father to call for free public schools under the Constitution. [7] In an educational policy paper he authored in 1791, Rush gave a dozen reasons why the Bible would never be taken out of schools in America. [8] He warned what he foresaw to be the results of removing the Bible from schools: an explosion of crime. He said:

> "In contemplating the political institutions of the United States [and he is pointing out the consequences of removing the Bible from schools], I lament, that we waste so much time and money in punishing crimes and take so little pains to prevent them." [9]

Benjamin Rush knew that if religious standards were removed, there would be no restraints on misbehavior.

Founding Father Noah Webster offered a similar warning. While we often think of him as an educator, he was a Founding Father, serving not only as a soldier during the Revolution, but as a legislator in Connecticut, Massachusetts, and even as a judge; and he was responsible for Article 1, Section 8 of the U.S. Constitution. In a textbook he authored for students, [10] he identified the reason that serious social problems might befall America:

> "All the miseries and evils which men suffer from vice, crime, ambition, injustice, oppression, slavery, and war, proceed from their despising or neglecting the precepts contained in the Bible." [11]

The Founding Fathers were very specific: they did not want any separation of religious values or religious principles from public life, for religious principles were the source of too many benefits for society.

President John Adams made the importance of these principles very clear in an address to the military on October 11, 1798. [12] In that address, Adams explained that there was no government in the world large enough to force people to do something against their will; you just cannot coerce good behavior. Adams pointed out:

> "We have no government armed with power capable of contending with human passions unbridled by morality and religion. . . . Our Constitution was made only for a moral and religious people. It is wholly inadequate to the government of any other." [13]

John Adams—whose signature appears on the Bill of Rights and the First Amendment—knew that our Constitution would only work for those people who could control themselves by religious values and religious standards. The Founders never envisioned any separation of religious principles from public affairs; they simply wanted a prohibition on the establishment of a national denomination.

President George Washington in his "Farewell Address" made an almost identical warning. For over a century, Washington's "Farewell Address" [14] was printed as a separate textbook because of its singular importance; students were taught that Washington's "Farewell Address" was the most significant political speech ever delivered by an American President. His "Farewell Address" was explaining to America what had brought her success and what would be required to continue that success. However, Washington's address is virtually unknown today and has not been seen in most American history textbooks in nearly four decades. Perhaps it is because of all the religious warnings Washington made in his "Farewell Address."

Certainly, George Washington was a Constitutional expert; he was president of the convention which framed the Constitution and he was the President of the United States who called for and oversaw the formation of the Bill of Rights and the First Amendment. Clearly, he understood the Constitutional intent and the meaning of the First Amendment. In his "Farewell Address," Washington explained that there were only two foundations for political prosperity in America: religion and morality—and that no man could be called an American patriot who tried to separate religion and morality from politics. As he declared:

> "Of all the habits and dispositions which lead to political prosperity, religion and morality are indispensable supports. In vain would that man claim the tribute of patriotism who should labor to subvert these great pillars." [15]

Washington continued with another warning—equally strong— reminding Americans that they should continue to reject any tenet which asserted that one could be moral without religion. That had been the premise of the French Revolution—and it had produced a bloodbath of executions and slaughters. In America, we knew better. Washington explained:

> "Whatever may be conceded to the influence of refined education on minds . . . reason and experience both forbid us

to expect that national morality can prevail in exclusion of religious principle." [16]

Washington understood that religion was the basis of morality and self-control and that morality and self-control were the only firm foundations of free governments. Then, in an almost rhetorical question, Washington simply asked:

"Where is the security for property, for reputation, for life, if the sense of religious obligation desert?" [17]

Washington knew that if we lost our religious principles we would not have any secure basis for property, life, or freedom.

When the Founders spoke positively of religion and its benefits, they were specifically referring to the general body of overall Biblical principles. This quote from Robert Winthrop, an early speaker of the House of Representatives, illustrates this. Winthrop said:

"Men, in a word, must necessarily be controlled either by a power within them or by a power without them, either by the Word of God or by the strong arm of man, either by the Bible or by the bayonet." [18]

It is evident from their writings that the Founding Fathers would never have tolerated the separation that we have embraced today. They knew that religious principles provided morality and self-control—the lifeblood for the survival of any self-governing community.

Since the phrase "separation of church and state" appears in no founding document, what, then, is the source of that phrase? And how did that phrase become so closely associated with and even become the defining metaphor for the intent of the First Amendment?

In 1801, the Danbury Baptist Association in Danbury, Connecticut, drafted a letter [19] to the President, Thomas Jefferson, arguing that freedom of religion was an inalienable right given by God—not government. They believed that for freedom of religion to even appear in the Bill of Rights was to cede to the government the power to regulate freedom of religion—a power they strongly felt that the government should not have.

On January 1, 1802, Jefferson wrote back explaining that there was no basis for their fear that the government would regulate religious exercise; for, as he said, the First Amendment had built "a wall of separation between church and state." [20] Jefferson further explained that man accounted for his faith and worship to God, not to the government, and that none of man's natural rights—the rights that he owed to God—would ever put him in opposition to or violation of his social duties—the duties that he owed to his government. [21]

Later courts expounded on Jefferson's letter. For example, in the 1878 case *Reynolds* v. *United States,* [22] the Court presented Jefferson's full letter—not just the eight words "a wall of separation between church and state" which is all most individuals today quote from his letter—but the Court presented Jefferson's letter and then summed up the intent of his phrase "separation of church and state" in these words:

> "Congress was deprived of all legislative power over mere [religious] opinions, but was left free to reach [only those religious] actions which were in violation of social duties or subversive of good order." [23]

The Court continued:

> "[T]he rightful purposes of civil government are for its officers to interfere [with religion only] when [religious] principles break out into overt acts against peace and good order. In th[is] . . . is found the true distinction between what properly belongs to the church and what to the state." [24]

According to the Court's understanding of Jefferson's letter, the government could interfere with religion only when its actions were "subversive of good order" or "broke out into overt acts against peace and good order." [25] That Court—and others (for example, *Commonwealth* v. *Nesbit* [26] in 1859)—listed representative actions into which—if perpetrated in the name of religion—the government had legitimate reason to intrude: things like human sacrifice, concubinage, incest, injury to children, advocation and promotion of immorality, etc.   But in all other orthodox religious practices— whether public prayer, the use of the Scriptures, etc.—the government was **not** to interfere. This was the clearly understood intent of Jefferson's letter and the way his phrase "separation of church and state" was applied for nearly a century and a half.

However, in 1947 a change occurred. That year, in the case *Everson* v. *Board of Education,* [27] the Supreme Court—for the first time in its history—used only the phrase, "a wall of separation between church and state." The Court did not give the context of Jefferson's letter and did not even show that previous Supreme Courts had used his letter to keep religious values and principles a part of society. That 1947 Court for the first time had used only Jefferson's metaphor—completely divorced from its context and intent.

Then, in 1962 in the case *Engel* v. *Vitale,* [28] that Supreme Court proceeded to re-define the meaning of the word "church" in the phrase "separation of church and state." For 170 years, the word "church" in that phrase had meant a federally established denomination. But in 1962, the Supreme Court explained that the word "church" would no longer mean a federally established denomination; it would now mean a religious activity in public.

With the Court now saying that "separation of church and state" was a prohibition against public religious activities, America was set on a new course. Under that new definition, many rulings have been delivered which violate not only the intent, but have even declared many activities unconstitutional which were the regular practices of the Founding Fathers themselves!

For example, in the case *Stone* vs. *Graham,* [29] the Supreme Court ruled that—under "separation of church and state"—it was unconstitutional for a student in school to even <u>see</u> a copy of the Ten Commandments, because—as the Supreme Court pointed out:

> "If the posted copies of the Ten Commandments are to have any effect at all, it will be to induce the schoolchildren to read, meditate upon, perhaps to venerate and obey the Commandments. This ... is not a permissible ... objective." [30]

According to the Court, to obey the Ten Commandments—things like "do not steal" and "do not kill"—would be to obey religious teachings at school, and surely the Founding Fathers would never have wanted students to be exposed to such teachings at school!

While this logic seems absurd, this is typical of the decisions in numerous similar cases which have been handed down since the re-definition of the word "church" in 1962. Over the last three decades, there have been some 6,000 cases in court which challenged religious expressions in public. Dramatic societal changes have followed the Court's prohibition of the teaching of long-standing religious values—and the changes were exactly what the Founding Fathers predicted.

Recall that both George Washington and Fisher Ames (the author of the First Amendment) warned that morality could not be maintained without religious principles; under the re-definition of the First Amendment and the misapplication of Jefferson's metaphor, it is now evident that we have lost our morality. For example, notice teenage pregnancies and how high they have soared since the removal of religious values. They had been low for decades; but now—since 1962—there has been over a 500% increase. [31] Every moral measurement shows the same statistical departure [32]—no religious principles, no morality.

The same is true with crime: since the Court felt that students might obey the Ten Commandments if they saw them, the Court prohibited students from seeing them at school. Notice that since the removal of religious principles, violent crime has increased 794% faster than the population growth. [33] Yet recall that Benjamin Rush predicted that if we were ever to take the Bible out of schools, we would experience a crime explosion. We were forewarned by the same men who gave us our founding documents; now we are experiencing the accuracy of their predictions.

Fortunately, however, current courts are slowly returning to the original meaning of the Founding Fathers; they are beginning to reinstate things which had been struck down in the past 30 years. For example, according to the Supreme Court decision *Westside* v. *Mergens,* [34] it is now permissible to have prayer and Bible clubs back on public school campuses. This Court understood what the Founding Fathers wanted: not a separation of religious principles or values, simply a prohibition on the national establishment of any particular religion.

Another area where the Court has re-allowed religious values is that of student morality; statistical differences can now be seen. In recent years, some courts had ruled that it was unconstitutional to teach pre-marital sexual abstinence in schools. [35] Along with the Ten Commandments, the courts reasoned that you could not teach absolutes because they were ultimately based on religious standards. However, in 1981, Congress—in an effort to reduce the extremely high teen pregnancy rate—passed the Adolescent Family Life Act which offered federal grant money to any group which would teach pre-marital sexual abstinence. [36]

When that Act became public law, it was challenged and taken into the courts. In the case *Kendrick* v. *Bowen,* [37] the lower courts ruled that abstinence was a religious teaching and to teach it to students would violate the Constitution. However, five years later when the case reached the U.S. Supreme Court, [38] the Supreme Court—while conceding that abstinence was indeed a religious teaching—reversed the lower court decision and ruled that since abstinence teaching was probably in the best interest of the students, it could be taught. Since that ruling, nearly a dozen major curriculums whose main emphasis is pre-marital sexual abstinence have been reintroduced into public schools. [39] Has that made any difference?

In the years when the courts would not allow the teaching of absolutes, the sex-ed from those years is categorized as "comprehensive sex-education material." In this material no "rights" or "wrongs" are presented. Students are simply told all the different possibilities of what can be done sexually in any culture around the world—no matter how extreme or abhorrent—and then encouraged to make their own choice. In essence: "It is your life—you live it! Do not let anyone tell you what is right or wrong." Sixty percent of students attending sex-education courses presently go through this comprehensive sex-education material. [40]

Currently, for every 1,000 girls in public schools who go through a comprehensive sex-education curriculum, 113 become pregnant. [41] However, in some of the abstinence curriculums, for every 1,000 girls in public schools who go through that curriculum, only 4 become pregnant. [42] This is a dramatic statistical difference, but it is because of the inclusion of the basic religious principles which teach traditional morality and self-control.

Similar positive statistics are now evident in obscenity enforcement (that is, the regulation and removal of adult-oriented type businesses and bookstores). In the recent Supreme Court decision *Barnes* v. *Glenn,* [43] the Court—in a reversal from the last 30 years—upheld the right of local communities and states to ban nude dancing. Nude dancing in recent years was called "free speech" or "free expression." However, this Court explained that nude dancing was not free speech and was not expression; it represented conduct; and conduct can be regulated.

The Court used statistics to prove that in areas where there was no obscenity enforcement—that is, no moral rights and wrongs—that the crime rate and sexual assault rate were much higher. The Court explained, "Nude dancing encourages prostitution, increases sexual assault, and attracts other criminal activity," [44] and that—simply in the interest of fighting crime—it is not only permissible, but it is desirable to have moral standards—even though many may consider those standards to be religious standards.

There is even a renewed interest in our history. As more and more are discovering how many of the teachings of the Founding Fathers we have lost, many are taking steps to correct that deficiency. The Kentucky legislature recently passed a law which encourages teachers in every school district in the state to re-post the teachings of the Founding Fathers—even if those writings have significant religious content. [45] The new law prohibits content-based censorship of American history due to the religious references in those documents. Teachers may now post Washington's "Farewell Address," previous Supreme Court decisions, and many other historical documents which previously had been excluded solely because of their religious content.

Historically speaking, including Biblical principles was the intent of the Founding Fathers; statistically speaking, including Biblical principles in societal programs has positive effects. Our Founders recognized that Biblical principles would treat the root causes of many of the surface problems which plague our society today. Our nation will only be morally strong to the degree that we return to the Biblical principles which were understood by our Founding Fathers.

Take courage, and stand up for what has been proven to be successful. Do not be fearful of utilizing Biblical principles or Biblical values, not only because they were constitutionally intended and are now being slowly reaffirmed by the courts, but especially because Biblical principles work!

EDITOR'S NOTE: A note about the difference in usage between "Court" and "court" should be made. "Court" (capital "C") refers to the Supreme Court of the United States, whereas "court" (lower-case "c") indicates a State Supreme Court or any other court, whether federal or state. Similarly, "Courts" specifically refers to the decisions of collective U. S. Supreme Courts and "courts" refers to the judiciary in general, represented by its jurisdictions from the lowest level local courts through the Supreme Court of the United States.

Footnotes

1. David Barton, *The Myth of Separation* (Aledo, TX: WallBuilder Press, 1992), p. 27, quoting *Annals of the Congress of the United States—First Congress* (Washington, D.C.: Gales & Seaton, 1834), Vol. I, pp. 420-914.

2. *Id.*

3. *Id.*

4. *Id.*

5. Fisher Ames, *Notices of the Life and Character of Fisher Ames* (Boston: T. B. Wait & Co., 1809), pp. 134-135.

6. *Id.*

7. Benjamin Rush, *Essays, Literary, Moral, and Philosophical* (Philadelphia: Thomas and William Bradford, 1806), see "A Plan for establishing Public Schools in Pennsylvania and for conducting education agreeably to a Republican form of Government," p. 1.

8. *Id.*, see "A Defence of the Bible as a School Book," p. 93.

9. *Id.*, p. 112.

10. Noah Webster, *History of the United States* (New Haven: Durrie & Peck, 1832).

11. *Id.*, p. 339, ¶ 53.

12. John Adams, *The Works of John Adams, Second President of the United States*, Charles Frances Adams, ed. (Boston: Little, Brown, 1854), Vol. IX, p. 229. See also *Revolutionary Services and Civil Life of General William Hull* (New York: D. Appleton & Co., 1848), pp. 265-266.

13. *Id.*

14. James D. Richardson, *A Compilation of the Messages and Papers of the Presidents, 1789-1897* (Published by Authority of Congress, 1899), Vol. I, p. 220, September 17, 1796.

15. *Id.*

16. *Id.*

17. *Id.*

18. Robert Winthrop, *Addresses and Speeches on Various Occasions* (Boston: Little, Brown, & Co., 1852), p. 172, from his "Either by the Bible or the Bayonet."

19. Letter of Oct. 7, 1801 from Danbury (CT) Baptist Association to Thomas Jefferson, Thomas Jeffrson Papers, Manuscript Division, Library of Congress, Wash., D. C.

20. Thomas Jefferson, *Jefferson's Writings*, Merrill D. Peterson, ed. (NY: Literary Classics of the United States, Inc., 1984), p. 510, January 1, 1802; see also *Reynolds* v. *U.S.*; 98 U.S. 164 (1878).

21. *Id.*

22. Barton, *Myth*, p. 43, quoting *Reynolds* v. *U.S.*; 98 U.S. 145 (1878).

23. *Id.*

24. *Id.*

25. *Id.*

26. *Commonwealth* v. *Nesbit*; 84 Pa. 398 (Pa. Sup. Ct. 1859).

27. *Everson* v. *Board of Education*; 330 U.S. 1 (1947).

28. *Engel* v. *Vitale*; 370 U.S. 421 (1962).

29. *Stone* v. *Graham*; 449 U.S. 42 (1980).

30. *Id.*
31. David Barton, *America: To Pray or Not to Pray* (Aledo, TX: WallBuilder Press, 1991), pp. 31, 32.
32. *Id.*, pp. 30, 34, 35, 37-41, 47-50, 87, 93, 96, 100-106.
33. *Id.*, p. 87.
34. *Westside* v. *Mergens*; 496 U.S. 226 (1990).
35. *Kendrick* v. *Bowen*; 657 F. Supp. 1547 (D. D. C. 1987).
36. *Id.*, p. 1552, *Adolescent Family Life Demonstration Projects, U. S. Code,* Vol. 42, Sections 300z-2 – 300z-3 (1981).
37. *Id.*
38. *Bowen* v. *Kendrick*; 487 U.S. 589 (1988).
39. Dinah Richard, *Has Sex Education Failed Our Teenagers?* (Colorado Springs, CO: Focus on the Family Publishing, 1990), p. 85.
40. *American Teens Speak: Sex, Myths, TV, and Birth Control* (Planned Parenthood Federation of America, Inc., 1986), poll conducted by Lou Harris and Associates, Inc. p. 50, see also a December 1, 1987 letter from the U. S. Dept. of Education reviewing the 1986 Poll.
41. Richard at 71.
42. *Id.*
43. *Barnes* v. *Glen*; 115 L. Ed. 2d. 504 (1991).
44. *Id.* at 522.
45. General Assembly, Commonwealth of Kentucky, SB 193, March 30, 1992.

Price List

Prices subject to change without notice
Quantity and case-lot discounts available

WallBuilders, Inc.
P.O. Box 397
Aledo, TX 76008
(817) 441-6044

Books & Publications

	Price/Copy	Quantity	Total

America: To Pray or Not To Pray? — $6.95
A statistical look at what has happened when religious principles were separated from public affairs by the Supreme Court in 1962.

The Myth of Separation — $7.95
An examination of the writings of the Framers of the Constitution and of the Supreme Court's own records.

The Bulletproof George Washington — $4.95
An account of God's miraculous protection of Washington in the French and Indian War and of his open gratitude for God's Divine intervention.

The New England Primer — $5.95
A reprint of the 1777 textbook used by the Founding Fathers.

Bible Study Course—New Testament — $4.95
A reprint of the 1946 New Testament Summary text used by the Dallas Public High Schools.

What Happened in Education? — $2.95
Statistical evidence that disproves several popular educational explanations for the decline in SAT scores.

Did Television Cause the Changes in Youth Morality? — $2.95
This exam is very enlightening not only as to what happened in television, but when it happened, and why?

Educ. and the Founding Fathers Booklet (See video) — $2.95

America's Godly Heritage Transcript (See video) — $2.95

Foundations of Amer. Government Transcript (See video) $2.95

Cassette Tapes

"America's Godly Heritage" (See video) — $4.95

"Education and the Founding Fathers" (See video) — $4.95

"The Spirit of the American Revolution" (See video) — $4.95

"The Laws of the Heavens" — $4.95
An explanation of the eight words in the Declaration of Independence on which the nation was birthed.

"America: Lessons from Nehemiah" — $4.95
A look at the Scriptural parallels between the rebuilding of Jerusalem in the book of Nehemiah and that of America today.

"The Founding Fathers" $4.95   _____   _____

  Highlights accomplishments and notable quotes of prominent Founding Fathers which show their strong belief in Christian principles.

"Keys to Good Government" $4.95   _____   _____

  The Founding Fathers formula for good government.

"8 Principles for Reformation" $4.95   _____   _____

  Eight Biblical guidelines for restoring Christian principles to society and public affairs.

"The Myth of Separation" (See book) $4.95   _____   _____

"America: To Pray or Not To Pray" (See book) $4.95   _____   _____

Video Cassette (VHS)

America's Godly Heritage (60 min.) $19.95   _____   _____

  This clearly sets forth the beliefs of many of the famous Founding Fathers concerning the proper role of Christian principles in education, government, and the public affairs of the nation.

Education and the Founding Fathers (60 min.) $19.95   _____   _____

  A look at the Bible-based educational system which produced America's great heroes.

Spirit of the American Revolution (53 min.) $19.95   _____   _____

  A look at the Christian motivation of the founders throughout the American Revolution.

Foundations of American Government (25 min.) $9.95   _____   _____

  Surveys the historical statements and records surrounding the drafting of the First Amendment, showing the Founders's intent.

Tax (TX only, add 7.75%): _____

Shipping (see chart at left): _____

TOTAL: _____

Shipping and Handling

Under $5.00	$1.50	$25.01-$ 40.00	$5.95
$ 5.01-$15.00	$2.95	$40.01-$ 60.00	$6.95
$15.01-$25.00	$3.95	$60.01-$100.00	$9.95

Canada orders add $5 extra.

* When shipping products to multiple addresses, please calculate shipping cost based on the dollar amount to each address—not on the order total. Thank you.

Please allow 4-6 Weeks for delivery.

"You see the distress that we are in . . . come, let us build the walls that we may no longer be a reproach." Nehemiah 2:17.